P.K. Page

# C O A L *and Roses*

Twenty-One Glosas

The Porcupine's Quill

Library and Archives Canada Cataloguing in Publication

Page, P. K. (Patricia Kathleen), 1916–
    Coal and roses / P. K. Page. – 1st ed.

Poems.

ISBN 978-0-88984-314-1

    I. Title.

PS8531.A34C63 2009        c811'.54        C2008-906935-8

1  2  3  ·  11  10  09

Published by The Porcupine's Quill, 68 Main Street, PO Box 160,
Erin, Ontario NOB 1TO. http://porcupinesquill.ca

Represented in Canada by the Literary Press Group.
Trade orders are available from University of Toronto Press.

We acknowledge the support of the Ontario Arts Council and the Canada
Council for the Arts for our publishing program. The financial support of
the Government of Canada through the Book Publishing Industry
Development Program is also gratefully acknowledged. Thanks, also, to
the Government of Ontario through the Ontario Media Development
Corporation's Ontario Book Initiative.

To you, my readers, whoever you may be

# Contents

The glosa form opens with a quatrain, borrowed from another poet, that is then followed by four ten-line stanzas terminating with the lines of the initial passage in consecutive order. The sixth and ninth lines rhyme with the borrowed tenth. Glosas were popular in the fourteenth and early fifteenth centuries among poets attached to the Spanish court.

Robert Penn Warren was born in Kentucky, in 1905. He was educated at Vanderbilt, the University of California, Yale and Oxford as a Rhodes Scholar where he received his B.Litt. in 1930. He published sixteen volumes of poetry, of which two were awarded the Pulitzer Prize. 'Treasure Hunt' appeared in *Incarnations: Poems 1966–1968*. Warren also published criticism, biography and ten novels, one of which (*All the King's Men*, 1946) also won the Pulitzer Prize and was made into a film that won an Academy Award for Best Picture in 1949. He died in 1989.

ROBERT PENN WARREN

# The Search

*Hunt, hunt again. If you do not find it, you*
*Will die. But I tell you this much, it*
*Is not under the stone at the foot*
*Of the garden, nor by the wall at the fig tree.*

    – Treasure Hunt

**Y**ou have the whole garden to search in.
    So begin. Begin now. Look behind every
shrub, turn up stones if
necessary, dig deep in the black
soil. Do not let night
interfere. Use a lamp to
light the darkness up.
There is no time to lose if
you are to succeed, so
*hunt, hunt again. If you do not find it, you*

may be sent to 'Coventry'.
Not pleasant.
No joke. But worse
is indeed possible. So look.
If you need glasses put
them on. Now. In that
way you should not even miss a bent
stalk. I cannot really
talk, nor mention what
*will die. But I tell you this much, it*

is not where or what you think –
in the woodshed, for instance, and not
behind the wheelbarrow nor in
the compost. Don't
waste your time
thinking where you would have put
it, had you been asked. You
weren't asked. But it – let me assist
you this much in your pursuit –
*is not under the stone at the foot*

of the broad-leafed maple. So stop
your wild surmises.
Time is running out and,
as your life
depends upon finding
it, search meticulously.
And good luck, I'd like you to
succeed.
Remember, not in the greenery
*of the garden, nor by the wall at the fig tree.*

Margaret Cavendish, Duchess of Newcastle (1623–1673), was an English aristocrat who became an attendant to Queen Henrietta Maria and travelled with her into exile in France, living for a time at the court of the young King Louis XIV. Cavendish was a poet, playwright, philosopher and essayist who published under her own name at a time when most female writers preferred to publish anonymously. Often controversial, she both criticized and engaged with members of the Royal Society of London and with the philosophers Thomas Hobbes and René Descartes. Fascinated by the discovery of the atom, Margaret's poem 'Of Many Worlds in this World' considers the notion that the world is made up of many smaller, complete entities. Her romance, *The Blazing World*, is recognized as an early example of science fiction.

MARGARET CAVENDISH

# Infinite Regression

*Just like unto a **Nest** of **Boxes** round,*
***Degrees** of sizes within each **Boxe** are found.*
*So in this **Worlde**, may many **Worldes** more be,*
*Thinner, and lesse, and lesse still by degree;*

— Of Many Worlds in this World

O nce in a bathroom in a rich hotel –
all mirrors – I descried myself reflected,
naked in mercury, and multiple –
recurring endlessly, each smaller me
retreating to a vast infinity.
It was as if the largest me was cloned
and then shrunk step by step. I barely saw
the final smallest me. It was too small.
That final smallest me could not be found –
*just like unto a **Nest** of **Boxes** round,*

or like those brightly painted Russian dolls
nesting within each other, large to small,
brought by an uncle from a far-off place –
a present for a nephew or a niece.
A wonder for that child – as Russian as
beluga caviar! There in her hand
Babushka in her headscarf with her brood
hidden within her, all identical
in everything but stature. Self-contained.
***Degrees** of sizes within each **Boxe** are found.*

This – 'infinite regression'. What a phrase
to conjure magic with! More to – in fact –
de-magic it, destroy it, make it flat
and merely physical when what it is
is metaphysical, a mystery.
'Regression' seems a grim and grey machine
designed for counting thumbtacks with, or nails,
from large to small, forever – endlessly.
*So in this* **Worlde** *may many* **Worldes** *more be.*

Molecule, atom, quark, neutrino. What
liberties I take with scale. Forgive
me, quantum physicists. Allow a fool
to simplify what that dead Duchess knew –
the weight of atoms and the large and small –
in Newcastle, a female prodigy,
before her time, intelligent, astute
observer of magnitudes – gross to minute
and so, to Absolute Infinity.
*Thinner and lesse and lesse still by degree.*

Gerard Manley Hopkins (1844–1889) was educated at Balliol College, Oxford, where he read classics. He converted from Anglicanism to Roman Catholicism in 1866 and subsequently chose the austere and restrictive life of a Jesuit priest. Hopkins' career choice also persuaded him to destroy much of his early poetry as he judged it incompatible with the rigour of his vocation. The language of Hopkins' poems is often striking. His imagery can be simple, or it can be lavishly metaphysical and intricate, as in 'As Kingfishers Catch Fire' in which one image leaps to another to demonstrate that each separate thing possesses its own uniqueness, and yet divinity reflects itself through all.

GERARD MANLEY HOPKINS

# Each Mortal Thing

*Each mortal thing does one thing and the same:*
*Deals out that being indoors each one dwells;*
*Selves — goes itself; myself it speaks and spells;*
*Crying Whát I dó is me: for that I came.*

    *— As kingfishers catch fire …*

**E**ssence, inner being, soul, heart's core,
   quiddity (poor thesaurus!) — are they one?
each other's twin, perhaps? — I doubt it. Heart
and soul? O, surely, one the flesh and one
the ghost of flesh, less heavy but more dense.
And yet their object, their intent, their aim
sprung from that inner being, arrowing
truly towards its target, is become
singular and centred as a flame.
*Each mortal thing does one thing and the same.*

Cat is only cat and I — though a myriad
selves are self — am never more or less
than is my essence. Surely 'ís is ís'
(and here I quote Frank Scott, who said it first)
and ever shall be, while osmosis-like,
I occupy — or is it? — am this flesh.
A mystery. Sometimes the Holy Ghost
seems immanent, sometimes a vacant house
spills out its emptiness, expels, expels,
*deals out that being indoors each one dwells.*

How focus and define it? Is there need?
Not for most selves, host selves, but for those
lightweight stragglers who stand about,
shadowy figures, who are part of it
unthinkingly, and have a need to see
intrinsically, be drawn in to their self –
their 'heart and soul' self – Freud would call it 'id' –
indelible as India ink, the stuff
of inward/outward self that spills and spills
*self – goes itself; myself it speaks and spells.*

A naked child, there in its very buff,
unspeaking still, is in its heart of hearts
itself – no other – has no either/or.
Its 'I am I' is printed in each cell.
And Rilke's 'tiny creatures' and great Blake's
innocent little Joy are both at home
in skin and every skein of DNA.
That self, that essence, singular, unique
knowingly enters in its place and time
*crying Whát I dó is me: for that I came.*

Ted Hughes (1930–1998) was an English poet, dramatist, critic and short story writer widely considered to be one of the best poets of his generation. Hughes graduated from Pembroke College, Cambridge, in 1954 then moved to London, where he worked as a zoo attendant and gardener. His first collection, *The Hawk in the Rain,* was published in 1957 to considerable acclaim. Fascinated by shamanism, hermeticism, astrology and the Ouija board, Hughes found in animals an apt metaphor for his view of life as a constant struggle for survival. He succeeded John Betjeman as British Poet Laureate and served from 1984 until his death. 'Creation' is a later work that appeared in *Tales from Ovid* (1997).

TED HUGHES

# The Age of Gold

*And the first age was Gold.*
*Without laws, without law's enforcers.*
*This age understood and obeyed*
*What had created it.*

    – Creation

**W**hat was, before the world
no one can imagine
and then the Creator created
winds and skies and seas.
Earth, with its fruits and trees,
before the world was old,
blossomed in sweet profusion.
Fish and flesh and fowl
were, magically, manifold.
*And the first age was Gold.*

And man appeared, and woman
innocent, full of wonder.
Eden, one myth called it,
Paradise, another.
Whatever the name, it was
flawless, an age of glory,
golden, sun-filled, honeyed,
lacking both crime and cunning.
It was a consummate order –
*without laws, without law's enforcers.*

Day followed night, the sky
cloudless, the air sweet-scented.
Night followed day, the stars
bright – Orion striding,
Cygnus, the Southern Cross,
the Lesser Water Snake.
All in their proper places
linked to the earth and shining –
a cosmological guide
*this age understood and obeyed.*

Minerals, plants and all
animals and humans
behaved according to
their original design.
Birds in their flight and flowers,
trees multifoliate,
salt in the mine, and water –
each honoured and celebrated
harmonized with and trusted
*what had created it.*

Juan Ramón Jiménez (1881–1958) aligned himself with a group of *modernistas* who staged a literary revival of sorts in the wake of Spain's loss of her colonies to the United States in 1898. Jiménez was born in rural Andalusia. He studied law at the University of Seville, but did not practise. His early poetry, influenced by the German Romantics and by French Symbolism, is strongly visual and dominated by the colours yellow and green. 'Yellow Spring' is one exemplar from this early period, which gave way to a later, more ascetic style dominated by white, after 1914. Jiménez fled Spain for Cuba in 1936 to escape the ravages of the Spanish Civil War. He was awarded the Nobel Prize for Literature in 1956.

JUAN RAMÓN JIMÉNEZ

# Ah, by the Golden Lilies

*... ah by the golden lilies,*
*the tepid, golden water,*
*the yellow butterflies*
*over the yellow roses ...*

    – Yellow Spring (translator unknown)

Jiménez, but for the roses
   you paint a Rio garden
   where every golden morning
the golden sunlight spills
on my Brazilian breakfast –
coffee like bitter aloes
strawberry-fleshed papayas
the sensuous persimmon ...
My young head full of follies
*ah, by the golden lilies.*

Beneath the cassia boughs
where fallen yellow blossoms
reflect a mirror image
I barefoot in the petals
trample a yellow world
while small canaries flutter
over the lotus pond.
I trail my golden fingers –
for I am Midas' daughter –
*in the tepid, golden water.*

My blue and gold macaw
laughs his demented laughter
dilates his golden pupils –
a golden spider spins
a spangled golden web
for beauty-loving flies.
Above the cassia branches –
the cassia-coloured sun.
Above the yellow lilies –
*the yellow butterflies.*

Jiménez, I am freed
by all this golden clangour.

Jiménez, your roses
denote a falling sound
a sound that will not rhyme
with *sambas jocosos*
*macumba, feijoada*
Bahían *vatapá.*
A different sun disposes
*over the yellow roses.*

e e cummings was born at Cambridge, Massachusetts, in 1894. He was educated at Harvard where his studies introduced him to the work of Gertrude Stein and Ezra Pound. He served as a volunteer ambulance driver in the First World War and was mistakenly interred on suspicion of espionage by the French. After the war, he divided his time between Connecticut and Greenwich Village, with frequent trips overseas. He travelled widely throughout Europe, meeting poets and artists, including Pablo Picasso, whose work he particularly admired. He died in 1962. His poem, 'somewhere I have never travelled, gladly beyond,' presents an impassioned defence of love, nature and the individual. It first appeared in *ViVa* (1931), a collection in which cummings pushes the limits of his characteristic scrambling of diction, syntax and typography.

E E CUMMINGS

## Your Slightest Look

*your slightest look easily will unclose me*
*though I have closed myself as fingers,*
*you open always petal by petal myself as Spring opens*
*(touching skillfully, mysteriously) her first rose*

       *– somewhere I have never traveled, gladly beyond*

ogether in a restaurant, at a party,
     where I have never traveled gladly –
or in the evening, listening to disasters
on national newscasts hourly and/or reading
scaremongering headlines in the evening paper,
arguing over politics and/or poetry
whatever we are doing, doing daily
moderately attentive, inattentive –
if I should glance your way, observing closely,
*your slightest look easily will unclose me.*

No matter if I sleep, my dream will see you
looking my way, the curious gaze you give me
bringing you to me bringing us both together
as if I were between you, you between me
in a sweet lovers' bow knot, and/or double,
our twoness only one, our twice-times single
as two eyes in a face, two hands together,
as two halves of a peach, and/or an apple.
I swear that – this my love song, I the singer –
*though I have closed myself as fingers*

are folded in a sleeping fist, and lazy,
my song continues in unspoken ways –
in images and/or surrealist music
in landscape, seascape, skyscape and/or air
until you break it with your laser eye's
accurate and/or unerring focus.
And I awaken with luxurious slowness
still soft from Morpheus – a drowsy flower
(yours for the picking, yet unpicked, and/or unbroken)
*you open always petal by petal myself as Spring opens*

crocus and aconite. A slow uncurling
from bud to brightest full-face turned to heaven.
I do not know the chemistry of bodies
yet know no other hands, and/or no lips,
which can so capably and quite uncurl me
outward, you-ward, into your embrace.
You are the world's blue skies and/or its rain
you are sweet-scented blossoms in a fervour
but most of all you are a summer breeze
*(touching skillfully, mysteriously) her first rose.*

Wallace Stevens (1879–1955) was born in Reading, Pennsylvania. He was educated at Harvard and then later at New York Law School where he graduated in 1903. Stevens is remarkable as a poet whose main output came at a fairly advanced age. 'The Man with the Blue Guitar', for example, was published in 1937, possibly after Stevens saw Picasso's painting 'Old Guitarist', from the artist's melancholy blue period. Stevens spent much of his adult life in the service of the Hartford Accident and Indemnity Company. He was awarded the Pulitzer Prize in 1955, and subsequently a faculty position at Harvard but declined on the grounds it would have required him to relinquish his vice-presidency of the Hartford.

WALLACE STEVENS

# The Blue Guitar

*They said, 'You have a blue guitar,*
*You do not play things as they are.'*
*The man replied, 'Things as they are*
*are changed upon the blue guitar.'*

    – The Blue Guitar

**I** do my best to tell it true
    a thing exceeding hard to do
or tell it slant as Emily
advises in her poetry,
and, colour blind, how can I know
if green is blue or cinnabar.
Find me a colour chart that I
can check against a summer sky.
My eye is on a distant star.
*They said, 'You have a blue guitar.'*

'I have,' the man replied, 'it's true.
The instrument I strum is blue
I strum my joy, I strum my pain
I strum the sun, I strum the rain.
But tell me, what is that to you?
You see things as you think they are.
Remove the mote within your ear
then talk to me of what you hear.'
They said, 'Go smoke a blue cigar!
*You do not play things as they are.'*

'Things as they are? Above? Below?
In hell or heaven? Fast or slow...?'
They silenced him. 'It's not about
philosophy, so cut it out.
We want the truth and not what you
are playing on the blue guitar.
So start again and play it straight
don't improvise, prevaricate.
Just play things as they really are.'
*The man replied, 'Things as they are*

are not the same as things that were
or will be in another year.
The literal is rarely true
for truth is old and truth is new
and faceted – a metaphor
for something higher than we are.
I play the truth of Everyman
I play the truth as best I can.
The things I play are better far
*when changed upon the blue guitar.'*

Dionne Brand is a prolific poet, novelist, filmmaker, educator and an influential human rights activist. She was born in Trinidad in a village called Guayguayare and emigrated to Toronto in 1970 where she attended the University of Toronto and the Ontario Institute for Studies in Education. Her poetry is characterized by formal and linguistic experimentation, which attempts to articulate the experience of immigrant women of colour in Canada. *Land to Light On* won the Governor General's Award for poetry in 1997 and *thirsty* was shortlisted for the Griffin Prize. *Inventory* is a long poem, published in 2005, that tallies the physical and emotional impact of globalization entailed by 'the militant consumption of everything'.

DIONNE BRAND

# soft travellers

*some words can make you weep,*
*when they're uttered, the light rap of their*
*destinations, their thud as if on peace, as if on cloth,*
*on air, they break all places intended and known*

    – Inventory

**t**here is magic, of course, and among the many magics there are
    words – spellbinders, but there is also sleight-of-hand,
and the magic of herbs, which perhaps a shaman
knows for healing, words
do not necessarily heal, they as easily arouse or wound
even when unspoken, their mere thought can cause hope
or despair to enter your poor heart
cowardly lion behind your rib cage,
some words can put you to sleep
*some words can make you weep,*

some without warning can make you laugh out loud or stun
you into silence, deafen or
dumb you
their abracadabra can weave spells
change matter, make manna of it
it is as if words were
physical, which of course they are, sound waves,
they are not emotional, in themselves,
but I suspect they care
*when they're uttered, the light rap of their*

consonants, their vowels in place
their very spelling important to them, I feel sure
they have their morphology as
you do, they insist
behind closed doors, felt-lined,
on tilde and circumflex, that there is worth
in orthography and there is worth
in geography as well – for words, that is
words correctly spelled have, in truth,
*destinations, their thud as if on peace, as if on cloth*

is so quiet, so light the heart could turn to stone
from such unbearable lightness
only shamans can know the magic of weights
only shamans the exact order of letters in a name or a place,
how to spell them right
and when the words have flown
as if they were birds
or a child's kite with a tail on a string,
or when they float down
*on air, they break all places intended and known*

John Ashbery was born in Rochester, New York, and raised on a farm near Lake Ontario. He attended Harvard, then subsequently completed a master's degree at Columbia in 1951. Though controversial, Ashbery has received nearly every major American award for poetry including the Pulitzer Prize for *Self-Portrait in a Convex Mirror* (1975). In his *Selected Prose*, Ashbery does not dispute a characterization of himself as 'a harebrained, homegrown surrealist whose poetry defies even the rules and logic of Surrealism'. 'Paradoxes and Oxymorons' was published in a collection called *Shadow Train* (1980). The poem acknowledges that even the closest of lovers can, and do, misunderstand one another, then questions the assumption that language can ever be an effective tool for the communication of ideas.

JOHN ASHBERY

# How to Write a Poem

*This poem is concerned with language on a very plain level.*
*Look at it talking to you. You look out a window*
*Or pretend to fidget. You have it but you don't have it.*
*You miss it, it misses you. You miss each other.*

    – Paradoxes and Oxymorons

It is raining and you've decided you are going to write a poem.
    What else is there to do besides phoning your mother?
And you don't feel like it not because you don't like your mother
in actual fact you love her and phone very often
but right now you have decided you are going to write a poem
and this poem will be a poem that you hope will be special.
Nothing symbolic or complicated, simple words, and language
a child could understand, but not a poem for children
with a moral and the struggle of good over evil.
*This poem is concerned with language on a very plain level.*

You are ready to begin. You have sharpened your pencil
the paper is lined in blue and is quite a bright yellow.
Listen to the poem talk, hear the words come together
and write them slowly and clearly so you can read them later.
This is the easy part, like taking dictation.
You must be deaf to long words like 'crescendo', 'diminuendo',
or cross them out if they surface, they are not for this poem,
and avoid scientific terms, botanical names or medical,
and a musical vocabulary – 'accelerando', 'glissando'.
*Look at it talking to you. You look out a window*

44

to avoid the poem's glance, turn away, embarrassed
by the poem and the fact that you're not fully attentive.
You are thinking of the rain that is beating with fury
against the dirty glass. You are thinking about everything
except the poem – about the gutters overflowing,
and is the cat in? But the poem begs you to give it
more than you are giving. The poem is expecting
your total attention. When it talks, you must listen.
Don't look abstracted – (O scribe, you must love it) –
*or pretend to fidget. You have it but you don't have it.*

It's not easy to focus. Perhaps the plain language
is what makes it so difficult. This poem's elusive –
a flirt, comes and goes, takes back what was given.
(There are phrases that describe it but you don't want to use them.)
Now the wind has come up and the cedars are blowing,
the garbage lids flying like frisbees and either
the roof's sprung a leak, or you left the tap running.
The paper's still empty, the poem unwritten.
You would have done better to have talked to your mother.
*You miss it, it misses you. You miss each other.*

Don McKay was born in Owen Sound and grew up in Cornwall, Ontario. He was educated at the University of Western Ontario in London and the University of Wales, where he earned his doctorate in 1971. McKay is the author of twelve books of poetry and has twice won the Governor General's Award, for *Night Field* (1991) and *Another Gravity* (2000). He has also won the coveted Griffin Poetry Prize for *Strike/Slip* (2006). McKay is an avid birdwatcher. Many of his poems are ecologically centred, inspired by the conflict between inspiration and the spirit, instinct and knowledge. In 2008, he was appointed to the Order of Canada 'For his contributions to Canadian literature as a nature poet and mentor of many emerging writers from coast to coast'. 'Edge of Night' appeared in *Camber* (2004).

DON McKAY

# Improbable Concept

*Certainly the dead watch us, but not*
*as opera, nor as the Great Grey Owl*
*tunes in gophers underground.*
*We are their daytime television.*

   – Edge of Night

**I**mprobable concept – the dead
     watching. Through pearls?
Empty eye-sockets?
Specially constructed binoculars, or more
improbable still,
through an interest in character and plot?
But why should they take to people-watching
rather than drywalling, glass-blowing
or manufacturing shot?
*Certainly the dead watch us but not*

daily. They can never know
when they'll be busy doing other things,
or falling asleep, dreaming
they jump rope among the asphodels
or climb Yggdrasil, the World Tree:
Or, perhaps, she – showered and cool –
prepares breakfast as usual
while he rolls over and yawns.
They don't watch us (or not as a rule)
*as opera, nor as the Great Grey Owl*

*Strix nebulosa*, the grey ghost
or phantom owl, who sees through his ears
or hears through his eyes or does
whatever is required for finding food
in the snow,
who makes no sound
beyond the whoooosh as he flies
and the whooo – ooo – ooo as he calls
and – unlike the yellow-eyed Great Horned –
*tunes in gophers underground.*

And we are certainly not opera for them because
the music of the spheres will drown out
Norman, Callas, Vickers, J. van Dam
and each and every note of Wagner's Ring.
But 'soaps' are under the radar
and, unless I am mistaken,
we are well cast,
act like pros, are word perfect,
and perform our parts with passion.
*We are their daytime television.*

Zbigniew Herbert (1924–1998) was born in the city of Lvov, Poland, which was annexed in 1939 by the Soviet Union, and then shortly thereafter by the Nazis. Herbert participated in the Polish resistance movement 'Home Army' during World War II. When the war ended he enrolled at the University of Cracow where he received a master's degree in economics. Later he earned a law degree from Nicolas Copernicus University and a degree in philosophy from the University of Warsaw. Place and history shaped much of Herbert's career as a poet. He lived most of his adult life under the ideologies of National Socialism and Communism. Not surprisingly, the infliction of the political on the personal informed almost all of his work. Herbert claimed the seventeenth-century English poet George Herbert as a distant relation.

ZBIGNIEW HERBERT

# Paradise

*Not many behold God*
*He is only for those of 100% pneuma*
*the rest listen to communiqués about miracles and floods*
*some day God will be seen by all*

— Report from Paradise  (Czeslaw Milosz and Peter Dale Scott, trs.)

Paradise is really the same as Britain
    There's the class system for instance
Some only just scraped in
through the celestial portals
Was it something about the accent
the diphthongs perhaps or vowels
the cut of the jib or jacket
not quite *quite*
Even though they are good
*not many behold God*

For God cannot hobnob
with any old Tom, Dick or Harry, God cannot
be expected to pass the time
(He has none to waste
what with the heavenly choirs to hear, the wings to evaluate)
for each and every newcomer
much as He might wish
Just where does He draw the line
anyway? according to rumour
*He is only for those of 100% pneuma*

while those of 90%
check their barometers daily
hypochondriacs of the soul
eager (so near!) to be nearer
while the 99-percenters
are you might say the bluebloods
and if not aristocrats at the very least 'county'
and soon to be elevated
from the could-bes to the shoulds
*The rest listen to communiqués about miracles and floods*

and are content for the moment
to be there, to have made it
for after all, the options –
not exactly a Sunday school picnic –
are Purgatory like a negative not yet printed
or the famous flames of Hell
So they are patiently happy just to have been accepted
and though there is no date yet,
and when, no one can tell,
*some day God will be seen by all*

Philip Stratford (1927–1999) grew up near Sarnia and lived for many years in Montreal, where he enjoyed a distinguished career as an academic and poet. A pioneer translator of Canadian literature, and especially the work of Antonine Maillet, Claire Martin and Robert Melançon, Stratford was the founder and first president of the Literary Translators Association of Canada. His own poetry included *The Rage of Space* (1992) and *Seven Seasons* (1994). *And Once More Saw the Stars,* written together with P. K. Page, (2001) is an unfinished sequence of four poems based on the Japanese *renga* as adapted by Octavio Paz and Charles Tomlinson.

PHILIP STRATFORD

# Domain of the Snow Queen

*This is the winter garden. White on white.*
*Bunches of snow like cherry on the bough.*
*Ground cover – icing sugar, flour or salt.*
*The pupils of my eyes have turned to milk.*

– And Once More Saw the Stars

**I**ce curtains on the windows, flowers and stars
etched for the Snow Queen, crystalline and cold.
Her blood subzero. See, how white her face,
how white her fingernails, her lips, her eyes.
Imagine then her heart, a block of ice
unmelting, permafrost. She whitens night
and everything she looks at – red or black
is bleached of colour by her frigid glance.
Even the rainbow is a pale delight.
*This is the winter garden – white on white.*

Her kingdom knows no summer, no warm breeze
stirs or disturbs its landscape, when it blows
it is an acid wind, corrosive, cruel.
But she is beautiful, her icy smile
would capture any child, her ermine robes
promising warmth. Her world of snow
sweet as marshmallows. How a child could eat
the landscape bit by bit, lie on his face
nibbling, chilling – blissed until he die.
*Bunches of snow like cherry on the bough*

make imitation springtime if he squints
his eyes just so, while drifts of lilies spill
and fill the little hollow near the hill.
But that is an illusion, what is true
is endless winter, view it how you will.
Although he eat it, it will never melt.
The fear: that he may sleep and never wake –
the snow so sumptuously soft and white.
The danger: that it may become a quilt.
*Ground cover – icing sugar, flour or salt*

for pastry cooks, a heaven till they learn
there is no pot or pan, there is no heat
no means of cooking, not for all their skill.
An empty promise, like the Snow Queen's kiss.
Everything is deception in this place,
even the snow – false snow that's made of chalk.
Where soot has fallen or where dogs have walked
white shifts its whiteness slightly but the sun
shines coldly down on yards of whitest silk.
*The pupils of my eyes are turned to milk.*

Gwendolyn MacEwen (1941–1987) was a unique Canadian novelist and poet. Her first published poem appeared in *The Canadian Forum* when she was just seventeen. She left school the following year to concentrate on her writing. Eyes outlined with kohl, often dressed in an embroidered purple tunic and writing of places far away, of magic, cats and demon lovers, MacEwen seemed to many an exotic and mesmerizing presence. She won the Governor-General's Award in 1969 for her poetry collection *The Shadow Maker*. She won the same award again in 1987 for *Afterworlds*. In less than twenty-six years, she published twenty books and became, with Margaret Atwood, the most celebrated poet of her day.

GWENDOLYN MacEWEN

# My Chosen Landscape

*I am a continent, a violated geography.*
*Yet still I journey to this naked country,*
*to seek a form which dances in the sand.*
*This is my chosen landscape.*

    – Finally Left in the Landscape

**S**and dunes, interminable deserts, burning winds
    the night temperatures bitter, a land of grit;
and floating above me stars as violent
as fire balloons, tactile and brilliant.
The all-enveloping sky, a cloak of soot.
This is my story, my brief biography.
The sum total of my experience. I travel –
a compass useless in my useless hand –
through a sandscape, a singular topography.
*I am a continent, a violated geography.*

Restless in all this emptiness, I seek
a fellow traveller, search for a sign –
a secret handshake, a phrase, some unusual colour
like periwinkle, for instance, or bright citrine,
but the monotony of sand persists
and nothing improbable finds entry
into the appalling platitudes of speech –
the *lingua franca* of everyone I meet –
in this land devoid of flags and pageantry.
*Yet still I journey to this naked country,*

for something in its nakedness has a beauty
so pure it is as if I thrust a knife
into my immaculate flesh and drew it forth
without a drop of blood being spilled. It is
abstract and invisible as air
this empty geometry, this ampersand
upon ampersand that leads me on
as if I were zero or the minus sign,
through 'and' and 'and' and 'and',
*to seek a form which dances in the sand*

But nothing formal dances. Only the wind
blows – unchoreographed – a floating ghost
across the dunes. The sand molecular,
airborne and free, is faint with the scent
of absolute dryness, a small mineral smell.
And this almost scentlessness, this shape without shape
is a violated country, one in which
I am both exile and inhabitant
and though I would escape
*this is my chosen landscape.*

In addition to the short stories for which he is most famous, Jorge Luis Borges (1899–1986) also wrote poetry, essays, prologues, criticism and reviews, and he employed two very unusual literary forms: the literary forgery and the review of an imaginary work. Borges was born in Buenos Aires and brought up in Spanish and English. He is reputed to have translated Oscar Wilde's story 'The Happy Prince' into Spanish when he was nine, perhaps an early indication of his prodigious talent. Although blind from a young age, Borges became head of the National Library. Borges' own translator, Anthony Kerrigan, has observed that a fundamental theme in his work is that of his own identity. 'Like Don Quixote, he does not mind being a character in a book, so long as it is in the *right* book and not the *wrong* one.' The poem 'Limits' appeared in *Jorge Luis Borges: A Personal Anthology* (1968).

JORGE LUIS BORGES

# The Last Time

*There is a line of Verlaine I shall not recall again,*
*There is a nearby street forbidden to my step,*
*There is a mirror that has seen me for the last time,*
*There is a door I have shut until the end of the world.*

– Limits  (Anthony Kerrigan, tr.)

J have been an omnivorous reader, cereal boxes
when I was a child at breakfast, comic strips
and all those stories in the *Girls' Own Annual*
that arrived at Christmas year after year and then
historical novels, Henty and Hugh Walpole
(and let me not forget 'The Little Red Hen'!)
Soon I shall not remember in any detail –
the Arabian Nights, the Russians or D.H.L.
When shall I totally not remember? When?)
*There is a line of Verlaine I shall not recall again.*

Everything slips away. The street I lived on
at the first address I ever learned by heart.
And all those years in barracks, teenage travels
England, Spain, and Fatima's Hand on doors.
The mysterious foreign world unfolded for me.
And places closer to home. Now their time is up.
Do they miss my footfall? My eager foolish heart?
Not only the streets of New York, the streets of London
and not only the path that leads uphill to the top,
*there is a nearby street forbidden to my step.*

And then there are mirrors in which I am forgotten.
Until puberty I was like a cat or dog
unable to see myself, but vanity came
with adolescence – 'does that ear stick out?'
And later, 'Am I beautiful enough to please him?'
And later still, 'My anti-wrinkle cream
is a total disaster.' I am grey, without lustre.
I refuse to look at myself in any glass.
Though I tell myself old age is not a crime,
*there is a mirror that has seen me for the last time.*

When will the end of the world, its trumpets blaring,
uplift the holy and take them home to heaven?
And what of us, the wicked, who were not taken?
Don't ask. There are a multitude of answers
all of them known to hospitals and prisons.
Shall I lie with my nails painted, my hair curled
awaiting my beloved, as of old?
Will darkness snuff me out in the blink of an eye?
or shall I, like Jorge Luis Borges, see only gold?
*There is a door I have shut until the end of the world.*

As a child, Theodore Roethke (1908–1963) spent much of his time in a large greenhouse owned by his father and uncle in Saginaw, Michigan. The glasshouse came to be his 'symbol for the whole of life, a womb, a a heaven-on-earth'. Roethke graduated from the University of Michigan and then later took a few graduate classes at Harvard, but abandoned his studies for financial reasons in the Depression. His first book, *Open House* (1941), was critically acclaimed on publication. He went on to publish sparingly but his reputation grew with each new collection, including *The Waking* which was awarded the Pulitzer Prize in 1954. 'In a Dark Time' appeared in *The Far Field* (1964).

THEODORE ROETHKE

# No Exit

*Dark, dark my light, and darker my desire.*
*My soul like some heat-maddened summer fly,*
*Keeps buzzing at the sill. Which I is I?*
*A fallen man, I climb out of my fear.*

     – In a Dark Time

*T*he Dark Night of the Soul, the darkest night.
        There is no darker. 'Pitched past pitch', he said –
Hopkins, that is. And Saint John of the Cross
knew equal suffering – a loss of faith
that nothing equals, so they say, but I
who lost my life – why can I not compare
my loss with theirs? Life is no little thing –
your own life or the life of a beloved.
The sun goes out, the moon. There is no fire.
*Dark, dark my light, and darker my desire.*

I wander disembodied in a void.
No body. Nobody. A curious thought.
A soul without its flesh is lost. A ghost.
Its bearings gone. It isn't even hell
it wanders through, but some drear desolate space,
silent, still, where 'no birds sing' and I
am dumb, and deaf to any natural sound.
What is this wasted landscape? this un-place?
what is this fleshlessness? A travesty.
*My soul like some heat-maddened summer fly*

circles the light bulb, circles the room, the world.
Circles forever – round and round and round.
Caught in a Möbius strip. No hope. *Huis clos.*
There is no other universe than this.
Nor heaven above it. This is terminal.
Poor soul, poor weary soul – point three three three
recurring endlessly. Monotony
fuels its tiny motor. Half asleep
it still asserts itself. I, I, I, I,
*keeps buzzing at the sill. Which I is I?*

As long as I can ask that question, I
exist, I live, but with no 'I', I am
nothing at all – not dead but like a flame
snuffed out, extinguished, finished, ended, done,
waiting a match to light its wick again.
And then a speck that glimmers on the air –
no gold, no diamond shines with such a light.
Some superhuman splendour fills my heart.
Awake once more I rise from my despair,
*a fallen man, I climb out of my fear.*

Marilyn Bowering's first novel, *To All Appearances a Lady,* was a 1990 New York Times Notable Book selection. Her second, *Visible Worlds,* was shortlisted for the prestigious Orange Prize and nominated for the Dublin IMPAC Prize. Marilyn Bowering was born in Winnipeg and raised in Victoria, B.C. She has travelled widely, and lived for a time in Greece, Scotland, Spain and the Queen Charlotte Islands. She has published fourteen books of poetry, two of which were nominated for the Governor General's Award. 'Love Poem for My Daughter' appeared in *The Alchemy Of Happiness* (2003). Bowering's latest novel is *What It Takes to Be Human* (2006).

MARILYN BOWERING

# On a Far Shore

*The night unravels its blue wool:*
*you stand on a far shore*
*about to set sail –*
*where are you going?*

> – Love Poem for My Daughter

**J**t is summer, early evening
    stars beginning
no dog barking.
The Morning Star
promises daylight,
and the moon is full.
Yet darkness fights for itself.
It has its methods,
is infinitely resourceful.
*The night unravels its blue wool*

from an endless supply
of old blue sweaters
fronts, backs and sleeves
right, left, the collar –
another sweater,
just one more
and then another
for insatiable night.
And you, obscure.
*You stand on a far shore.*

I try to see you through a glass.
You are almost invisible
a tottering spindle
alone and fearless
solitary, frail,
in some nameless country.
The next ship is yours.
You board with no luggage.
You lean on the rail
*about to set sail*

for who knows where?
Some unknown harbour?
I would travel with you
but you won't ask me.
Nor will you tell me.
The wind is blowing
and you are a leaf
in a springtime gale.
There is no knowing.
*Where are you going?*

Federico García Lorca is, arguably, the most important Spanish poet and dramatist of the twentieth century. Lorca was born in 1899, in Fuente Vaqueros, a small town not far from Granada. In 1919, he moved to Madrid, where he became part of a group of artists known as Generación del 27, which included Salvador Dalí and Luis Buñuel. Despite the poet's claim that he himself did not understand the poem, 'Somnambule Ballad' tells the story of a wounded gypsy smuggler seeking refuge from the Guardia Civil. The poem appeared in *Romancero Gitano* ('The Gypsy Ballads'), 1928, which was Lorca's first commercial success. Lorca was murdered by Franquist soldiers in 1936, at the start of the Spanish Civil War.

FEDERICO GARCIA LORCA

# Green, How Much I Want You Green

*Green, how much I want you green.*
*Great stars of white frost*
*come with the fish of darkness*
*that opens the road of dawn.*

– Somnambular Ballad  (Stephen Spender and G. L. Gili, trs.)

L andscape of crystals
    rock salt and icebergs
white trees, white grasses,
hills forged from pale metals
padlock and freeze me
in the Pleistocene.
See my skin wither
heart become brittle
cast as the Snow Queen.
*Green, how much I want you green.*

Green oak, green ilex
green weeping willow
green grass and green clover
all my lost youth.
Come before springtime
before the brown locust
come like the rain
that blows in the night
and melts to fine dust
*great stars of white frost.*

Water, sweet water
chortling, running
the chinooks of my childhood
warm wind, the ripple
of icicles dripping
from my frozen palace.
How sweet the water
moonstones and vodka
poured from a chalice
*with the fish of darkness.*

Come water, come springtime
come my green lover
with a whistle of grass
to call me to clover.
A key for my lock
small flowers for my crown.
The Ice Age is over,
green moss and green lichen
will paint a green lawn
*that opens the road of dawn.*

Thom Gunn (1929–2004) was born in Gravesend, Kent. He graduated from Trinity College, Cambridge, in 1953, the year before his first collection *Fighting Terms* was published. On graduation he was awarded a fellowship to Stanford University in California. Gunn subsequently lived nearly all his adult life in the city of San Francisco. From the late 1960s onward he owned one of the famous 'Victorian' houses in the Haight-Ashbury district, then at the peak of its notoriety. The themes of gay love and male companionship combine in Gunn's magisterial response to the AIDS epidemic of the late 1980s, which he published as *The Man with Night Sweats* (1992). 'The Wound' is an early work that appeared in *Fighting Terms* (1954).

THOM GUNN

# After Chaos

*The huge wound in my head began to heal*
*About the beginning of the seventh week*
*Its valleys darkened, its villages became still:*
*For joy I did not move and dared not speak.*

    – The Wound

**I** had been dealt a blow, a giant axe
    came crashing through my skull. But how explain
it wasn't physical, there was no blood
or bruising even, just a gaping hole,
a crater fashioned by some meteor
of the imagination. No, no axe,
now that I think of it, now I *can* think.
(My thoughts are gathering like gnats at dusk –
a thickening in the air. I shall be well.)
*The huge wound in my head began to heal*

as imperceptibly as water turns to ice.
The slow coagulation that I felt
was like a blessing – easeful, easeful bliss
forgiving me for something I had done
some unremembered, unimportant thing.
It would be weeks before my lips would speak
the words my mind was forming – Mumma, Da
or No, no, no or Give me, give me, *me* –
one's first attempts at language. When I spoke,
*about the beginning of the seventh week,*

my climate changed, and my whole continent
suffered a seismic shift, tectonic plates
in offshore waters made a break for it
and I was earthquake country, one vast shake
and then the aftershock and then the quiet
that follows chaos. Now I would be well.
The healing had begun. I felt each cell
working with every other cell, a truce
throughout my kingdom, it was peaceable.
*Its valleys darkened, its villages became still,*

great cities lost their lights and it was sweet
beneath the pyrotechnics of the stars.
Pre-birth perhaps before the soul puts on
its skimpy flesh, before the mind acquires
the warps and woofs that fashion it for earth.
I wondered if the whole thing was a joke –
gods playing us like any other game?
Then knew I didn't care. I was a dot
in some celestial pattern we all seek.
*For joy I did not move and dared not speak.*

Anna Akhmatova (1889–1966) was born Anna Gorenko in Odessa, Ukraine. Her father disapproved of her early interest in poetry and forced her to use a pen name for which she adopted the last name of her maternal great-grandmother. Akhmatova attended law school in Kiev and married Nikolai Gumilev, who was executed in 1921 by the Bolsheviks. There was an unofficial ban on Akhmatova's poetry from 1925 until 1940, during which time she wrote a long poem, *Requiem*, dedicated to Stalin's victims. In 1965 she earned an honorary degree in Literature from Oxford. 'Everything Is Plundered ...' appeared in *Anno Domini MCMXXI* (1922). Akhmatova died in 1966 in Leningrad, where she had spent most of her life. A minor planet, discovered in 1982 by the Soviet astronomer Lyudmila Karachkina, is named after her.

ANNA AKHMATOVA

# Coal and Roses – A Triple Glosa

*Everything is plundered, betrayed, sold,*
*Death's great black wing scrapes the air,*
*Misery gnaws to the bone.*
*Why then do we not despair?*

    – Everything is Plundered … (Stanley Kunitz and Max Haward, trs.)

I.    **J** read the papers with my morning coffee.
        Only the horoscope columns offer hope.
We sell our birthright piecemeal to our neighbour.
Our natural resources are going, going, gone –
our oil, our gas, our water, clear-cut forests.
We dynamite glaciers in our greed for gold.
Polar bears, seeking ice floes, swim and drown.
The pillars of our society are felons.
To those of us who knew a more innocent world,
*everything is plundered, betrayed, sold.*

How many children, this week, shot their mothers?
How many mothers drowned their two-year-olds?
Car bombs account for many, cluster bombs.
Madmen shoot up classrooms, shoot themselves.
This week's body bags again outnumber
the body bags of last week. Who can bear
those plastic-wrapped, young, beautiful, rigid corpses
shipped to their grieving girlfriends, pregnant wives?
My armband weeps, I weep, and everywhere
*death's great black wing scrapes the air.*

Street people line the sidewalks, homeless people,
hands out, begging – the unemployable
with all hope gone. Go on, take a dare –
stare in those vacant eyes that gaze on nothing
but heartache, hunger, unimaginable despair.
His Honour, the Mayor of our bustling town,
complains they are ruining the tourist business,
their visibility – a mortal sin
against the holy dollar. O God, where have you gone?
*Misery gnaws to the bone.*

Prices go up and up. The rich are richer.
*La dolce vita* in every household, gourmet fare
ordered from gourmet takeouts. The new kitchen,
now an appliance showcase, gadgets galore,
high tech, electric. Hydro cuts a bagel!
Alarm systems only increase our fear.
What are we locking out? our kids on crack?
thieves with firearms? the all-enveloping dark?
Terrorism brandishes weapons everywhere.
*Why then do we not despair?*

*By day, from the surrounding woods,*
*cherries blow summer into town;*
*at night the deep transparent skies*
*glitter with new galaxies*

     – Everything is Plundered …


II.   **P**erhaps the crocus, with its furry presence
             pushing toward the sunlight through the snow
         offers us hope that the whole world is waking
and making music. Tulips, daffodils
narcissus, jonquils, hyacinths, all the bulbs
that paint the air and cram the flowerbeds
sweet-talk us into festival and folly.
By night, a fragrant vegetable scent
hovers above the new thin summer bedspreads.
*By day, from the surrounding woods*

bird calls sound. Nest building is beginning.
Fledglings will hatch and fly. The seasons turn
in ordered, immemorial procession.
Despite excessive rains, power cuts and winds
of hurricane proportions – this is spring:
the longed-for after-winter everyone
was dreaming during those dark months of waiting –
an alternate reality, a bright wing.
And suddenly the grass is overgrown,
*cherries blow summer into town*

and kids wear shorts and singlets, and pale girls
search out last year's sandals, part their hair
the other side perhaps, pubescent boys
buy after-shave and condoms. Everywhere
there is a shine, rain glistens, threads of sun
are weaving multicoloured tapestries,
spiders spin webs, even the dung beetle
dreams his own small wonderful dream of heaven.
By day the universe is like a kiss,
*at night the deep transparent skies*

carry us upwards, outwards, into space.
Lie on your back on cooling grass and stare.
Like Zeus, the Perseids shower us with their gold,
and 'Look'! we cry and 'Look'! They come so close
they almost touch us and their pale, cold fire
links us with heaven and the Pleiades.
Flesh is forgotten; gone the hoof and horn,
the claw, the canine teeth, the bitter blood
as overhead the deepening darknesses
*glitter with new galaxies.*

*And the miraculous comes so close*
*to the ruined, dirty houses –*
*something not known to anyone at all*
*but wild in our breast for centuries.*

     – Everything is Plundered …

III.    *T*here is a place, not here, not there. No dream
        nor opiate can conjure it – it is
not heaven, though heavenly – it is its own
element – not sea, not earth, not air,
nothing approximate, nor halfway matched,
where other laws prevail. It honours those
who enter it like water, without wish
vainglorious or trivial – a gift
from realms of outer unimagined space.
*And the miraculous comes so close*

it alters us. It is as if a beam
embraced us and transformed our molecules
and merged us with some cosmological
and fractal universe we never dreamed,
more vast than any thought we had of love
divine or secular, a synthesis
of right and wrong, of midday, midnight, dawn,
of poverty and wealth, sackcloth and silk.
A gift of coal and roses
*to the ruined, dirty houses*

and to their opposites – the shining palaces
floating above in towers of cumulus –
that take on size the way a child's balloon
can fill with breath, or perfume scent a room.
This beam – not tenuous or crystalline,
minus proportions, neither large nor small –
is all-encompassing, a kind of womb,
a 'heaven-haven' and improbable,
some entity beyond recall.
*Something not known to anyone at all.*

And yet it is our heartbeat, intimate
and human. Here, my wrist – its pulse
is yours for the taking, yet it is not yours.
We share a heartbeat, share lub-dub, lub-dub.
All races, genders, share that little drum
and share its Drummer and its mysteries.
This quiet clock, unnoticed day by day,
our ghost attendant, is invisible,
untouchable, perhaps sublunary.
*But wild in our breast for centuries.*

# Acknowledgements and Credits

To those friends who suggested quatrains, Théa Gray, Rosemary Sullivan and Rachel Wyatt, my thanks.

Some of these poems have previously appeared in the *Journal of Canadian Studies, Poetry, The Chicago Review, The Walrus, Prairie Fire, The Poetry Nation Review* (UK), *Poetry Northeast, Descant, Literary Review of Canada, The Malahat Review, Rocksalt* and the Canadian edition of *Dream Catcher*.

For permission to reproduce the photographs throughout the text, acknowledgements are due to the following:

– The Granger Collection, New York, for Federico Garcia Lorca, Robert Penn Warren, Jorge Luis Borges, Juan Ramón Jiménez and e e cummings
–The Huntingdon Library, San Marino, California, for Wallace Stevens
– Kari Reynolds for Gwendolyn MacEwen (photo by Mac Reynolds)
– National Portrait Gallery, London, for Gerard Manley Hopkins, Margaret Cavendish, Edward James (Ted) Hughes and Thomson William (Thom) Gunn (Fergus Greer, copyright holder)
– Michael Elcock for Marilyn Bowering
– John Haney for Don McKay
– Joel Meyerowitz Photography LLC for John Ashbery
– Bentley Historical Library, University of Michigan, for Theodore Roethke (U-M Alumni Association, Box #145, ROE, James O. Sneddon/photographer)
– Anna Beata Bohdziewicz for Zbigniew Herbert
– Anne Stratford for Philip Stratford
– Anna Akhmatova Museum, St. Petersburg, for Anna Akhmatova
– McClelland & Stewart for Dionne Brand (photo by Neil Graham)

# About P.K. Page

P.K. Page was born November 23, 1916, at Swanage, Dorset, England. In 1919 she left England with her family and settled in Red Deer, Alberta. She went to school in Calgary and Winnipeg and in the early 1940s moved to Montreal where she worked as a filing clerk and researcher. She belonged to a group that founded the magazine *Preview* (1942–45) and was associated with F.R. Scott, Patrick Anderson, Bruce Ruddick, Neufville Shaw and A.M. Klein. Her poetry was first published in *Unit of Five* (1944) along with that of Louis Dudek and Raymond Souster. From 1946 to 1950 Page worked for the National Film Board as a scriptwriter. In 1950 she married William Arthur Irwin and later studied art in Brazil and New York.

P.K. Page is the author of more than a dozen books, including poetry, a novel, short stories, essays and books for children. A memoir entitled *Brazilian Journal* is based on her extended stay in Brazil with her late husband who served as the Canadian Ambassador there from 1957 to 1959. A memoir in verse, *Hand Luggage*, explores in a poetic voice Page's life in the arts and in the world.

Awarded a Governor General's Award for poetry (*The Metal and the Flower*) in 1954, Page was also on the short list for the Griffin Prize for Poetry (*Planet Earth*) in 2003 and awarded the BC Lieutenant Governor's Award for Literary Excellence in 2004. She has eight honorary degrees, received the Order of British Columbia and is a Fellow of the Royal Society of Canada. She has also been appointed a Companion of the Order of Canada.

Painting under the name of P.K. Irwin she has mounted one-woman shows in Mexico and Canada and been exhibited in various group shows. Her work is represented in the permanent collections of the National Gallery of Canada, the Art Gallery of Ontario, the Victoria Art Gallery and many collections here and abroad.